I0410526

# The Bottom Feeders

# (Some call us white trash)

# by

# Gene Taylor

© 2004 by Gene Taylor. All rights reserved.

No part of this book may be reproduced, stored in a retrieval system, or transmitted by any means, electronic, mechanical, photocopying, recording, or otherwise, without written permission from the author.

ISBN: 1-4140-5883-7 (e-book)
ISBN: 1-4140-5884-5 (Paperback)

Library of Congress Control Number: 2004090336

This book is printed on acid free paper.

Printed in the United States of America
Bloomington, IN

1st Books - rev. 02/24/04

The Taylor family survived the 1930's and 1940's with many psychological scars but a strong belief in *God*.  Many Americans suffered along with them and were left with the same scars.  Those without a strong religious faith may still be suffering along with the generations that follow.

This book and my prayers are dedicated to all of them.

# Table of Contents

# PROLOGUE . . . .

As I pondered how to tell this story of a desperately poor Georgia family in the 1930's, I tried to envisage who may care and thought probably not many. The weight of that probability forced me to continue because I know someone should care. I realized there is a profound lesson in this story for all of us.

# THE BOTTOM FEEDERS

On a freezing February morning in South Georgia, the sun seemingly cannot rise as if held down by the ice in the air but sends glimmers of its struggle. Yet another struggle is going forth here this morning in 1937. A young mother and her five children are nestled inside an abandoned corn storage shack they call home, and indeed it is a very cold Georgia morning.

---

How the Taylor family found themselves in this desperate situation and how we endured is part of a tragic chapter in our history that for the most part has been denied. In the cities, the Great Depression was obvious. There you could see the homeless and the hungry in lines to get their soup and we knew they existed, where they were and how many had to be fed. The Government and the Churches mobilized as best they could to help them. But in the hills of Appalachia to the backroads of Alabama, Mississippi, Georgia, Louisiana, and Florida, far greater numbers were unemployed, near starvation and without medical care. These were people that were dirt poor <u>before</u> the depression. But then they could find day jobs weeding and planting crops for the farmers. Some were sharecroppers but if the total produced and sold is zero, there share is now zero. The farmers had no money for seeds and fertilizer, and the supply stores could not afford to grant credit for crops that could not be sold. A large segment of the south just came to a stop. Many folks have no income, no savings; landlords in desperation have evicted them. They live out in the county scattered along dirt roads and mountain trails in West Virginia and Kentucky. There was no welfare department anywhere near most of them. They were out of sight and little effort was made to find them. Local churches could have done more but they were poor, trying to survive themselves, and for the most part tried not to see them.

Despair is everywhere and it breeds hostility in men that cannot take care of their families. Some left to "go find work" and never returned. Maybe they left just so they would not have to look at the hunger in their children's eyes anymore. "Dam them!" "String up the bums!" you might say. But what you would do in these circumstances is not known. These were uneducated folks, probably averaging five or six years of formal education, and were not able to comprehend why any of this was happening. Not understanding the national economic problems, they viewed themselves as being the cause and could find no answer.

How did the Taylor family end up in an abandoned corncrib with a four year old (Gene), a five year old (Vince), a seven year old (John) and two girls,

Belle (thirteen) and Bobbie (nine), and the mother now alone with her children. How could we survive? How would this kind of fear and torture effect the physical and mental health of our family? Remember we are an example of thousands more throughout the south. One might wonder how another generation or two might be affected.

This morning in 1937, four months past due with the rent, out of lies to tell the landlord and sick with a hangover from drinking a fifty cents gallon of moonshine whisky this week, Oscar Taylor said goodbye to his family. We were mostly gullible enough to believe him when he said he was going to Orlando to find work. He was a barber by trade but business was very slow and someone had told him there were new houses being built in Orlando so he was going there to be a house painter. He had drank too much "shine" for years resulting in many bad times for the Taylor family but we had always had a house to live in and some food on the table.  That was about to change.


Things got worse fast - When the landlord learned that Oscar was gone and with him his last chance of collecting the back rent, he kicked us out - literally setting our meager belongings out into the yard.  Apparently the landlord had told my Mama's brother-in-law, Uncle Henry, about the situation and he came over to our house with a truck to help us.  I remember well that we got very little help over the years from any of our relatives on either side of the family. Mama said it was because they did not like Daddy because he drank too much and was a mean drunk.  Anyway, this time he had come to help. He had asked a nearby farmer if we could move into an old abandoned sharecropper shack that he now used to store dried corn for hog feed.  He had said that we could but we would have to push the corn over to one side to make room but that we could use it until we could do better.  Looking back now I have many times wondered how the Taylor Clan, some owned farms in the area, and

Mama's family, the Knights, who lived in the area and were doing pretty well, could have turned their backs on us like this. Uncle Henry at least came and moved us to the free shack he also found for us. Without him I suppose we would have just been walking down the road until someone let us in and we would have lost all our things, meager as they were. So we appreciated greatly his help. Times were hard and judging others is always difficult and better left to God.

We moved into the shack on the coldest day of my life. I was only four years old and you may think memories are not retained at that age but that is not true. Perhaps it depends on the gravity of the recollection. It was so cold when we were evicted from our home without warning that morning that I will never forget how it felt, how cold it was and how afraid we all were. What would happen to us and where would we go? The landlord told Mama he regretted what he must do but do it he must. He told her our Uncle Henry had promised to be here this morning to do something with us because he knew the landlord was putting our things out on the front yard, which was the eviction law. Imagine how cold and deserted we felt sitting out in the yard on a freezing winter day waiting on Uncle Henry to arrive. Mama kept saying "Thank God it ain't raining today. I don't think we could stand all this if it was raining too" she told us that as if it would make us a little warmer and she told the landlord the same thing two or three times as I recall as if to make him feel better for what he was doing. And she prayed to God out loud several times to help us in this day of great need. Finally, to the great relief of Mama and the landlord as well, Uncle Henry arrived. He was alone driving his old Ford pick-up truck. It took him three or four trips as I recall completing our move to the corn shack and he tried to put a good face on it for us all. He kept saying our Pa would be home soon and the old shack would hold us pretty well until then. He did not seem nearly as cold as I was and maybe his clothes were warmer. I did not know why but I just kept thinking how terribly cold it was and I sure hoped there was a fireplace in that shack we were being moved to today. He loaded up Mama's pots and pans first and our clothes and us kids on the first load so we could get out of the cold wind as soon as possible. I don't know why the pots and pans and the oil cook stove went first because we had ran out of kerosene, but I guess Mama figured we would get some later.

When we got to the shack and started pushing the corn from one side of the house, I vividly remember the large rats that shared the space with us. They did not bother us because they had plenty of corn to eat - But they had to worry about the huge snakes that lived under the house. We could see them through the cracks in the floor. We would lay on the floor with our eyes close to a crack to get a glimpse of a big rat snake looking for an errant rat. Strangely enough, it seemed that none of this devastated us at all. Mama kept telling us that life was good and we were all together and God would provide. Food, water, and heat were problems that had to be solved as if we were engaged in a survival course.

The shack had a working fireplace, so we gathered sticks and small branches from dead trees nearby to keep a fire going this very cold February. There was an open well and out-house in the back yard. We lowered a bucket on a rope down 15 or 20 feet and brought up water. At first it was nasty - dead frogs and other critters to be removed but eventually it was clear and drinkable. We had no choice - it had to be. Uncle Henry had given us a small supply of food from his panty to last a few days in the hope that daddy would be back soon. After a few days we began scavenging for food that the land could provide. Looking back, I think that God was providing but not making it too easy on us. The fields around us had Irish potatoes and sweet potatoes buried in the sandy clay soil that had been missed at harvest. They were few and far apart but could be found with a stick stirred around in the ground.  We roasted them in the fireplace coals at night for supper and for breakfast.

The shack was a typical share-croppers house situated on the far side of the farmer's land. Sharecroppers lived here until they gave up hope for continued survival and moved to town.  The farm was located several miles outside of Adele, Georgia on a rusty-red clay road.  Deep ruts in the road verified that mostly wagons pulled by mules had traveled it.  It was one half mile to the paved road that the school bus traveled.  Out here the farms were about two or three miles apart, with the sharecropper's house situated as far from the owner's home as possible.  Sharecroppers were usually Negroes or uneducated poor whites and the farmer did not want to live too close to them.  But in reality there was not much difference in them.  The farmer probably had little education himself and being the closest neighbor, they quite often became good friends. The sharecropper would help the farmer with his crops and the farmer would come over at various times and help the sharecropper with crops the sharecropper had planted. And so, to some extinct, they became more like partners in some of the better relationships.

The point is that neither had much when they planted in early spring and little more after the harvest. But hopefully they would have laid-away some canned vegetables, smoked pork, syrup, and meal for the winter months and dried corn and hay for the livestock. There were some wealthier farmers in the area but a very few. Many of these farmers received their land as Government grants and then struggled for years trying to keep them. Then other Government programs helped them to stay on the farm because the country needed them there but it effectively made sharecroppers out of them with the Government being the owner. So they did not really feel that superior to their sharecropper and in many instances were not.

We, of course, were not sharecroppers. We were just indigent interlopers that the farmer was willing to help temporarily but would like to see move on before he had more corn to store. He never came around to say hello or anything. Like many others, he tried not to see us.

My older siblings knew that the bus they rode to school came down the paved road one half mile from the house so they walked there in the morning to catch it. They continued on to school as if nothing was different. But things were quite different - they had no lunch. Mama had to iron their clothes by heating an iron in the fireplace coals at night and pressing the clothes with the heated iron. But they were always clean and wore pressed clothes to school. It is hard to imagine that the other children and the teachers at school did not know the plight of our family. Therefore, I must assume that it was almost normal for the times.

We survived. Try to remember here that we are in the United States of America and the Great Commonwealth of Georgia - not the Congo or Nigeria - and you will understand why I had to write this story. Maybe a politician or two or a church historian somewhere will shed a tear. Maybe not, but God knows what went on in the minds of our relatives and our neighbors and the church congregations in the area, and the governments in Atlanta and Washington.

But the really awesome part of this story is that we, as a family, not only survived but also we were happy! Yes, happy because we had a family and a mother and a father (although he was away looking for work at the time). We had faith that he would return and we had faith in God. And the potatoes were still coming up from the sandy clay fields.

Spring came slowly, almost begrudgingly, for our small band and brought several kinds of relief, but no daddy, no husband for mama, but warmer days and nights. John and Vince started fishing in a nearby creek every chance they had and I tagged along as well. They made fishing poles from tree twigs and line made from thread or string and the hooks were gold-colored safety pins from Mama's sewing box. The bait (earthworms) was plentiful. Those little "brims" would hit the gold pins sometimes even without the bait! So now we added fish to our menu. Life was good. All things are relative.

"Mama! Mama!" Vince called out from the front porch one Saturday morning, "Daddy's coming home - he's walking down the road with his suitcase". He walked on up and sat his suitcase on the front porch and announced "There really was not that much work down there in Orlando so I came on back home". Simple as that and now he is back. Almost no wonder, it seemed, as to how we had found food and survived while he was gone. Maybe he just assumed that Mama would take care of us somehow. And of course, he has right. Also

I think asking questions and talking about it could only show how wrong he was. So it was easier to just look over it like it didn't happen. So now someone else can't see us. But that is the way it is. He had a few dollars and he promised us he would look around for a better house to rent and maybe he could get his job back at the Barber Shop in Adele. Mama was happy he was back. She loved him no matter what all her family said about him, no matter he drank too much and deserted his family from time to time. We loved him too because he was our Daddy and the only one we had. Now he is back and life is good. We are a very happy family.

We moved to a rental house closer to town but still in the country. Everyone caught the same bus to school. We struggled along the rest of the year with enough food and clothing to get bye on, meager but sustainable. Christmas came and Mama was able to get enough money from Daddy to get each of us one gift. The boys all got a cap pistol and some caps, Bobbie and

Belle got new coats that they wanted. That is always what we got - one gift - and it was hard to come up with that.

Granddaddy Knight would come by when he knew Daddy wasn't home and leave us a basket of fruit and some hard candy. We never thought much about this being a small amount. Anything was appreciated.

And so this small band of survivors moved on with their lives. The strain of living through a depression continued. Then Mama told us she was pregnant with her 6th child in the spring of 1939. That's what we needed, another mouth to feed and she did not seem as healthy as before. Also I was sick with kidney and liver problems. Yellow Jaundice was diagnosed followed by kidney infections. My eyes would swell and close for days at a time. The doctor was concerned when I was five years old that I could lose my sight if I did recover. He thought however that I could recover over time but it went on like this for several months. Now Mama was pregnant and her health was not good, so we were being tried again. Our faith has been on trial before and would be many more times.

Claudia Belle graduated from high school in June of 1939 at fifteen years old and had made application to go to nursing school in Jacksonville Florida at St. Luke's Hospital and Nursing School. She had A's and B's in high school and this program only accepted the top students. She could work her way through being a nurse assistant in the hospital to pay the tuition. By the time Robert was born she had escaped. I do think that best describes her exit and her feelings at the time. See you later - I'm out of here! And we were all happy for her - especially Mama - although she could have used her help at this time.

Mama caught the bus to Valdosta with me a few times to see a specialist that the county would pay for. This was her first introduction to the welfare system. Until then, all through the tough years she had never had this kind of help. This was because we lived in the country and no one came looking for you. Then Robert was born sickly on September 1, 1939, almost died in the first few weeks, and would remain sickly most of his life. So, she was caring a heavy load at this time and with her own health failing. Now Daddy started acting bad again at this worst of all times. He started going missing for days, then weeks at times. There was no money for medicine for the sick children. Our desperate Mama started leaning more on the Welfare Department for help. Though the doctor treating the children, she was given medicine and baby food. Daddy resented this when he learned of it and ordered her not to take help from the Welfare Department. To him this showed that he was not capable of taking care of his family and it embarrassed him. She told him she had no choice and this further aggravated the situation. If he were living at home, they would limit this aid, but when he deserted us, they would help again. So it was on and off situation for awhile but finally the rent was past due and he had deserted again.

The Welfare Department counseled Mama that for the sake of the sick children, she needed to go on a full subsistence welfare program and offered to move us to Valdosta Georgia (20 miles) which was a bigger town with full welfare facilities. There we would find better doctors available to social services, food banks, etc. Adele simply did not have the full welfare facilities to help us but in Valdosta they could. The rules were that the family qualified as long as Daddy was not living at home and had in fact deserted his family. If he came back we would no longer receive assistance. He understood and accepted this plan without a problem and stayed away. And so it was that in October 1939 they had us and our belongings trucked to a rental house on the south side of Valdosta Georgia. On the "bad side" of the tracks we would learn later.

# THE MOVE TO VALDOSTA

We thought we had died and gone to heaven. We had part of a two-story house divided up into apartments. It was a clean, sound house, nice by most standards of which we were aware. It had an inside toilet, running water, electricity, and oil heat. There were lots of children in the streets that we had not been exposed to in the past and that worried Mama some. The next day after we moved in, as promised, the welfare agents delivered a box of food - bags of rice, beans dried peaches, grits, lard, and flour. We would not go hungry again! Mama studied the supplies and made up menus for us to ponder. Beans over rice with biscuits, peach cobbler and so on. It was like Christmas, and that was only the beginning. They also left us some authorization chits (handwritten coupons) to take to a bakery to get day old bread, Cinnamon buns, rolls and donuts. The following day was to become one of my fondest memories and a great adventure. We got up early in anticipation because

Mama had told us to go and find that bakery and get our bread and sweet rolls. John, Vince, and me started walking toward the north side of town where we had been told the bakery was located. We had a little red wagon that I can't recall where we got it, and we pulled it, taking turns and sometimes I rode. It was about four miles to that bakery but we were so excited it could have been four blocks the way we jumped and skipped along. We handed a baker on the loading platform our "chit" and announced that we had come to get some bread and donuts or whatever they might have to give to us. He was obviously overwhelmed with sympathy. Three little ragged boys with a red wagon to pick-up some welfare bread. He called out a couple of other workers to talk to us and help load our supplies. "Where do you live asked one. "Where did you move from?" asked another. "How many in your family" asked the third. We had never had so much attention and we were all trying to answer them and being as nice as we could be, not wanting to say or do anything that would effect our gift of free bread and donuts. And did they load us up! They stacked that wagon full as it could take with bread, then Cinnamon rolls, and donuts on top! We ate a lot of donuts on the trip back home but you could hardly miss them, we had so much. It will be hard for most folks to imagine the shear joy we felt upon acquiring all this good food. And I suppose it is a good thing that you cannot. As we walked back across town, now about noon, we did not care about how the folks sitting on their front porches in this more affluent section of town stared at us as we passed. We were probably a pretty interesting looking sight to them and they probably knew we didn't belong over here. We just thought they were envious that we had all that bread and donuts.

We came across a Piggly Wiggley Food Store along the way and we were really getting into the adventure now. For whatever reason, John and Vince decided to circle around to the back door to check out the garbage bins to see what they may be throwing away. Sure enough we found a bonanza, a quarter of a box of grapes turned about half brown but still very editable, and a half stalk of bananas also turning brown but still good to eat. We did not have room in the wagon but by unloading it and putting the wood box of grapes and bananas on the bottom we could re stack the bakery goods on top and acquire our additional treasures. Then it was Vince that got over into a large can where there was some freshly cut beef bones that had been trimmed and thrown out. Each had a small amount of meat missed by the butchers' knife - soup bones we would call them. They did not smell bad once removed from the garbage can, so we loaded them up too. We would later make many trips back to this garbage can. We were astonished that in this town they would throw away food this good.

When we got home, Mama was thrilled with our bakery goods and she along with Claudia Belle and Bobbie grabbed a donut or a Cinnamon Roll to try them out. She also was happy with the grapes and bananas and also amazed that they would throw away very good fruit like this that we had seen little of for a long time. The soup bones were a different matter and she chastised us for getting meat out of a garbage can. However she looked at it closely and smelled of it real good, then washed it off and put it in a pot of boiling water, added dried beans, and we had a wonderful supper with a loaf of bread on the side and Cinnamon Rolls for dessert! Life is good. All things are relative.

# THE SECOND PHASE OF POVERTY

The fall of 1939 found the Taylor's in a new apartment on the north side of Valdosta, the "*good side*" of the tracks. Mama had cried and begged the welfare department to get her family out of the southside where she was sure the children would become tainted by the dirty white trash that lived there.

The new apartment was the downstairs of a two-story frame house with another rental apartment upstairs. It was in a good location near the schools. We could all walk to school and it was near the Piggley Wigley Food Store and the bakery!

I refer to this as the second phase of poverty because it is important to understand that there are two distinct phases. The worst is rare in the United States but not so rare in Mexico, Cuba, Haiti, Africa, etc. That is the poverty of hunger, cold, homelessness, untreated illnesses, and complete hopelessness. That phase we escaped in 1939 when the welfare department moved us to Valdosta and gave us a chance. In my lifetime, from that day to this, I was never hungry again.

However, though out my lifetime from that day to this, I always feared that it could happen again! That is why to this day I want to get a case of canned tomatoes, beans, and corn in the pantry. To open the door and see them reminds me that I am not close to going hungry again, more than the Mercedes in the garage.

It is important to understand that this psychological impairment explains the dark forces that have driven my siblings and me all these years. It is why at six years old in the first grade of elementary school in a strange town,

I visited the bakery located just off the school grounds and asked them for a job. It was like I did not want to stop digging for potatoes. I had mentioned to one of my classmates how all of my family would like to find jobs to help out at home and he told me about the bakery and how sometimes they would let kids sell donuts after school. So off I went and asked for a job. They gave me a shoebox full of donuts (a dozen) and I sold them to housewives on the way home three for a dime. I had to give the bakery thirty cents when I returned, so I was making ten cents a day and walking straight home! Not bad for a six year old. It is interesting to me years later that I can not remember ever eating one of those donuts.

I continued over these first few years of somewhat improved prosperity to land other jobs. I washed dirty pop bottles, bleach bottles, etc. for a man that made roach poison in his kitchen and sold it door to door. He would buy old bottles from kids for half a cent each and pay me fifty cents to wash them all on Saturday mornings. And in season, I sold boiled peanuts on a street corner - Bobbie had a part-time job at McCory's Five and Dime. John and Vince both sold newspapers on the corner and other small jobs. Mama worked in the beginning at a Government sewing factory - which was a requirement under the welfare program. They had a nursery day care center for little Robert and for me before I started to school. She was sick a lot - I'm not sure what she had but she was not really well for long periods after Robert was born and was sickly as well. Some of it was physical and I think some of it was simply depression from the harsh treatment life had bestowed upon her. She came from a well-educated but not wealthy family that looked down on her now to some extent. They were all more prosperous and didn't have much to do with us. It all weighed heavily on her during these times beginning the second phase of our poverty.

All of this defines the psychological pains that must be endured as a poor welfare family. No stomach pains from hunger and no more crawling around in the sand looking for potatoes to keep from starving, but now you must interact with a society that looks down on you and wishes you were not there. It is a different kind of hunger and we are trying to dig and scratch our way up and out. Now it is the hunger for respect and equality and the pains would last for many years, perhaps for a lifetime for some of us. In the beginning it looks like we will easily make it because the gains are many and easy to attain. When you are waste deep in a hole and gain a foot it seems like a lot. Until you learn that a lot of people don't want you up there on the same level as they are on. It will get harder and harder over the years to gain any more ground. We thank God that we are not hungry and that we have been given the chance to try.

Our faith would be very important in the years to come in keeping us as a family on an even keel. Not one of us got into trouble with the law and we had our faith to sustain us when social injustices made life difficult. The Bible teaches that wealth and happiness are not necessarily entwined but poverty and happiness can be. We knew that our unrelenting love of God would bring us happiness on Earth or certainly in Heaven. Our Mother taught us this first and then the Presbyterian Church reinforced her teaching when we began attending the First Presbyterian Church of Valdosta. I began to realize that the "dirt" poor and the "filthy" rich had something in common. Neither was competing in a class struggle. As we began to improve ourselves a little, we found ourselves at the low end of a competitive ladder. Before, there was no competition because no one knew we existed. The pure happiness we experienced as a non-competitive *"Bottom Feeders Cast"* would never be accomplished again. Or would it? Can't we see the fallacy in this clash and ignore it, find happiness in our success and enjoy the rewards with no envy or bitterness towards others?

Looking back, I will always wonder at how happy our family was when living in a corn barn and scavenging for food. How could that be? Certainly no one would want to recreate that situation in a search for happiness, but we need to know why we lose it when we begin to compete with our neighbors, "the Jones". Some diminution of faith may be the answer. At this time our faith was strong - we contacted God in prayer and asked for deliverance and for our health and he gave us both. We clung together as a family and found happiness in that even though we had no material goods. And so I know happiness can be found at this low point if you face it with God and the Bible as your guide.

Mama and me started going to the Presbyterian Church and sometimes Bobbie, John, and Vince but mostly it was Mama and me. We seemed to have more of a fervent need for a religious connection, a guide to contact with the Lord, than did the others. That's not to say they were any less Religious, but they did not seem to need the church as much. The church was about a mile or so away and we could walk that. We went mostly on Sunday nights at first and then later to Wednesday night prayer meetings. We also loved to go to any "revivals" where the traveling preachers set up their tents and shouted their Hell and Damnation Sermons. Some were really great preachers and they had movie slides showing Heaven with its Golden Streets and Angels awaiting the righteous. Then they had films of the pits of fire and brimstone with the Devil awaiting the Sinners! After a couple of hours with them there was no doubt in my mind where I wanted to go! They were good and we always came up with a nickel or two for the offering. They gave us hope; "The meek shall inherit the earth," they would shout. There was no one meeker than we were. They always spoke harshly about the wealthy hoarding their gold and how they would not be welcome in heaven, and we knew it was true. It had to be.

In school I was an A and B honor roll student - mostly A's - and for seven consecutive years I received gold attendance certificates for perfect attendance. The perfect attendance impressed me more over time than the A & B Honor Roll because I wondered how I could have gone that long without the Mumps, Chicken Pox, etc. Either I had those things in the summers or Mama sent me to school with them. I think probably the latter. Mama always told us if we felt sick in the morning that we would feel better after we got to school. Actually it seemed to work! Years later I would look back on these times, as I would go several years without missing a single day of work. Attendance and work ethics are taught early in life and in my case by my Mama. And I have found as a manager of several businesses later in life that work ethics dictate success more than high school or college grades.

Something occurred early in my young life that

shocked me into the belief that nothing I could ever do or accomplish would make me an equal within the society I lived. That is a terrible feeling to live with, particularly if you are smart and excel in school, naturally industrious and work hard at all opportunities, and you are a Christian and attend church every week. Certainly you should be accepted and given opportunities to succeed and advance socially as well as financially. The occurrence I mention here would probably seem trivial to most casual observers, i.e., the children involved, the parents and the teachers involved, and not as the catalyst for a lifetime of fear and rebuke. My 2nd grade classmate, Jane Ebeshard was having a birthday party. She was my friend in the classroom and I was in the top two or three in the class in grades and generally well liked. When she passed out invitations at school for a party it appeared everyone was invited except me. Several kids asked me if I was going and I gradually became aware that most were invited. I was crushed. I went home and told Mama that I just could not understand this. She asked if I knew where she lived and I told her on the north side of town in a large home and that I thought her father was a lawyer. Mama said that I must also know why I could not be invited. She said she could attend public school with me but would never open that world to me.

"*White Trash*" was the name they gave us and I heard them occasionally say so, but for the most part it did not bother me. I always thought I could work my way up the ladder and be better than that some day. This is the day I knew that was not true. In Valdosta, Georgia I was always going to be *"white trash"*. It is hard to explain and harder to admit but I never to this day got over that omission of my name from that birthday party in the second grade.

Looking back now I see how the affluent white southerners detested the *"Bottom Feeders"* as an embarrassment to the white race - the obviously superior race except for those failures and misfits. We would continue to be the object of contempt because we were there and someone had to always be there which elevated them by comparison. That is how the cast system works. They also had contempt for the Negroes that lived in the area but it was not the same. They did not accept them as being in any way equal or acceptable and therefore did not feel contempt for them or anything else for that matter. But whites that lived like Negroes now that was something else. If the schools had been desegregated at this point in time, and I had been the only Negro in Jan Ebeshardt's class, then certainly I would have been omitted from the invitations and I think I would have probably expected as much being the only Negro in the class at that time. It would not have been right but I think I would have expected it.

But I was not a Negro and so this burned deeply into my psyche. It also gave me a lot of insight into the feelings of minorities. Many times I have thought that being a poor Negro might have been more comfortable during those times than being poor white trash. And I think *"Bottom Feeders"* better describes us because we were not trash but did scrape the bottom for survival and were not an accepted *"class"* of whites just as the *"untouchables"* were not accepted in India. But we did not have a *"class system"* in the United States. Did we? We had white *"Bottom Feeders"* and black *"Niggers"* and black *"Negroes"* if they had improved themselves somewhat. We had middle class hard working whites and the *"White Aristocracy"* whose families traced themselves to the plantation owners prior to the civil war. Some just claimed this heritage - God only knows where their wealth came from but no one questions them because of their wealth. They could be the most ruthless and overbearing. And some were not even wealthy but acted the part and had long noses.

I continued going to church as a more and more dedicated mission. I wanted to be close to God and I wanted something to make sense out of the disappointments and trials that life had placed before us. Our preacher, Reverend Cecil Thompson baptized Mama and me one Sunday and we became members of the First Presbyterian Church of Valdosta. It made me feel like I belonged to something. For sure I saw some of the same selfish people at the church but I thought there was hope for them as long as they came to church and listened to the Gospel. Preacher Thompson took me in as a kind of prodigy and for several years we were very close. I told him I wanted to attend the Presbyterian Seminary in Atlanta when I finished school and he promised to help me. I would visit his study after school many times, mostly on Wednesday afternoon before Prayer Meeting which Mama and me always attended. He would let me help with Sunday's sermon, which he would start working on Wednesday, and use some of it at prayer meeting. It was interesting to me how he would use current events in the news and the scriptures that had similarities or answers to the current problems. I knew then that was what I wanted to do with my life.

At Prayer Meeting I sat on the first row. He would explain to the congregation that he seated me there because I became enthralled with the sermon my legs started swinging and I would kick the pew in front, my legs being too short to touch the floor. They always laughed at that - although I recall him telling it several times. Then he would often call on me to stand and say a prayer and I enjoyed doing that. It made me feel like I was almost preaching. I read the Bible everyday and felt like I had read every line of it over time. Now I wonder why children are not introduced to daily Bible reading more. It would enhance their education by improving their reading skills and would encourage the reading of other books while giving them the strength found in faith. Religion during my youth was my guiding light.

I would then go through a period that changed

me from a devout Christian to an agnostic almost in the blinking of an eye. Or at least it would seem. These events were just a continuation of disappointments and failures for me to endure. I was chiseled and formed by them.

In December 1942, Claudia Belle came home from nursing school, pregnant with Rebecca Ann who would be born in June. Claudia had a brief marriage to James Ray of Jacksonville, Florida who was then drafted into the army and sent to England. It was not a happy marriage and he would not write or answer her letters. She was able to force him to participate in a monthly allotment check to her, which was a big help to our little band now that she was back home. Also she got a job with the A & P Food Store and would become a store manager after "Becky" was born. After the birth, she took the job of store manager in Quitman, Georgia about forty miles away. There she rented a room and came home every other weekend or so. Mama took care of Becky almost totally from the time she was born for about two years. She was just like a baby sister to me. With the increased money from the government allotment check we began to improve our situation somewhat.

Claudia was a strong domineering type - or at least compared to Mama, and more than Bobbie. The rest of us were just kids at the time and not involved. Claudia began to insist that Mama get a divorce from daddy and keep him away from the family. He would come around from time to time and stay a few days in violation of the welfare rules. If they found out, the welfare check would stop. Claudia did not want that to happen. Without it and if she should leave, we would be in a destitute situation again. So she wanted to finalize the situation by the divorce. Mama really did not want a divorce. It was bad for her self-esteem but was probably the right thing to do. She finally agreed and Claudia got a lawyer to handle it. She had also talked to the same lawyer about divorcing her husband "*in absentia*" which was allowed during the war years if a military man deserted his family by his actions. He would not communicate with her and the army could not council him to do so. They were eventually divorced. He had never seen Becky and never did as far as I know. The divorce between Mama and Daddy was also granted and she was to receive $10.00 per week child support. We received it sporadically over the years. Even occasionally was better than nothing.

In 1944 we were improved financially enough to look for a better house to rent with a little more room. We found one on the same street, closer to our church and in a nice neighborhood. Mrs. Kendrick owned it and the home next door that she lived in. She was a nice middle aged widow and pretty well off financially I thought. We all got along well with her and she was very reasonable with the rent. We rented the downstairs of a large two-story home upstairs she had four rooms for rent to gentlemen only.  The gentlemen renters had a private staircase so we did not see them and they were no bother to us.  Sometimes one of two of them would sit on the front porch in the evening and we would talk to them.  Eventually, Mama would meet one of them, Gus Mathis, and became friends.  Over many months she would talk to him and slowly a relationship ensued. Marriage would not come about until he was ready to return to Jacksonville, Florida and they did not want to part.  He had been living in one of the gentlemen rooms while working on a big construction job in Valdosta for a large plumbing company in Jacksonville.  He was a master plumber and a hard worker but just a poor man - no home or anything and was divorced also.

During the war years, the economy in Valdosta improved considerably.  Everyone seemed to be doing better.  Daddy worked at a barbershop and had a part-time job managing the barbershop at Moody Air Force Base just outside of town.  So he had good money coming in and paid his ten dollars per week child support pretty regularly. It was Vince's job to go to the barber shop every Saturday and collect it. So, with that and Claudia's money, and Bobbie also working, we were doing reasonably well. Dysfunctional, but eking out a living and gaining one of the lower rungs of society's ladder.

# THE FAMILY GROWS UP/
# DYSFUNCTIONAL AND AGNOSTIC

In the winter before I was twelve years old, my life began to change as reality clashed with my religious beliefs. In the beginning it seemed liked a rather innocent problem but it would forever change my life. Looking back I see this as a complicated prism with me entering the business world at a very early age. In another view, I see child exploitation with an adult working children who are underprivileged. I see children trying to go to school and perform many hours of work before the beginning of classes. However, I know that was not the intent of the adults involved in my story. It is just how it looks when viewed from a certain angle of the prism, but I was harmed by their actions, no matter their intentions. It seems so strange looking back that before I was twelve, I would be so torn and mentally strangled by such events.


It began when one of my school friends told me how he helped his Dad some mornings deliver papers. He would stop by their home after he got all his paper route boys started on their routes and get my friend to help him on his car route. He was looking for a full time boy for that job and was letting his son fill-in until he found someone. Mr. Bob, as everyone called him, was the Valdosta Distributor for the Florida Times Union and the Atlanta Constitution. I would learn later that the Negroes usually took the Florida Times Union. It was a fine newspaper but many took it because it contained a cartoon drawing called *"Hambone"* which supposedly had numbers hidden within the drawing that would be helpful in picking the winning Cuban Lottery numbers! Also the winning numbers would be shown after the weekly drawing in Havana if you knew how to read them within the sketch drawings. No where in the paper would any of this be mentioned but they all knew about it and did not want to miss an issue of the paper. There were lottery sellers in the community that sold the tickets and paid off for the Cuban Lottery each week to the winners. It was illegal but no one seemed to care. This activity continued all the years I lived in Valdosta.

I went to my friend's house after school to meet Mr. Bob and ask him for the job. He explained to me that the job was to stand on the running board of his 1939 Plymouth and help him deliver papers to a large scattered area too long for it to be a bicycle route. It would take two hours starting at 5:30 to complete that route but first we had to distribute the papers to each of the bicycle route boys and make a few drops of extra papers along some of their routes so, we had to actually get started at 4:15 each morning! Mr. Bob was a very big man - probably 300 lbs. And had difficulty getting in and out of his Plymouth, so he certainly needed a helper. He offered me the job at six dollars per week and breakfast which was two donuts and a cup of coffee or a glass of milk each morning before we started our route. I accepted the job and he told me to be sure my Mother understood that he would be at my house every morning at 4:15 sharp to pick me up. We would then meet with all the bicycle route boys at a gas station where the trucks from Florida and Atlanta unloaded Mr. Bob's papers. Mr. Bob and I would then count out the papers for each of the bicycle routes. When this job was complete, we would all go together to the White House Restaurant in the center of town just as it opened for the day. There we were served our donuts and coffee/ milk before starting our route. Some of the boys may buy more than their allotted breakfast but all would at least get their two donuts and they were as large as a coffee cup saucer. I think Mr. Bob knew these boys did not have much and wanted to know they got something before starting out in the morning.

All of this team work and being a part of something that had this much structure was appealing to me - and I needed the money. But the hours were very difficult while attending school and completing homework in the evening and going to bed early. There was little time left for anything else. But the really big problem I had was working on Sunday.

Sunday was our biggest day because the papers were much larger - more drops for the other boys - and we had to stop and collect from all the weekly subscribers and the Sunday only. Being a devout Christian, how could I work on the Sabbath and miss church? But I needed the money and it seemed to be a big challenge, something new to be a part of, like an extended family almost.

So I asked Mr. Bob if there was anyway I could be off on Sundays. He said, Sunday was his biggest day and he had to have me on that day. He told me to discuss this with my Mama. So I told Mama that I was troubled by the Sunday work because it was a sin and an affront to *God*. Remember now that I was only almost twelve years old and what pressure had been brought to bear on me. I felt like one of the money changers that *Jesus* threw out of the Tabernacle. But we needed the money and I had a chance to have a regular paying job. She told me to do what I thought was right but suggested that I talk to Preacher Thompson.

I went to the Preacher's study where I had been many times before Prayer Meetings and began to tell him my problem, my conflicts with the scriptures and my need for the job.

Now sixty years later I reflect on this and I know I put Preacher Thompson on trial to take my place before *God* and that was not fair - But remember I was not yet twelve years old. But I was old enough to know that working on the Sabbath was a sin. In my mind I knew what the answer was and what Preacher Thompson should tell me. He surprised me and disappointed me when he told me that *God* would understand if I took the job because my family needed the money. He said I could still come to Prayer Meeting on Wednesday and on Sunday nights and that would be just fine. He gave me a pragmatic answer - not a religious answer - not one founded in the scriptures. Now I understood how the rich were able to hoard their money while hundreds in their community went hungry. They have found a reason that justifies their actions and they come to church on Sunday and give some paltry sum to the church and find forgiveness for all their sins at least in their minds. The scriptures are for reading but not necessarily to be followed literally - just to whatever extent one pragmatically can.

I have said that I became an agnostic that day but to be factual, I now believe it was an accumulation of disappointments.  Long before I presented Preacher Thompson with my dilemma, I had suffered many long hours thinking about what I thought *Jesus* had taught us to do and the acceptable perimeters within which we must exist to be Christians.  I realize that none of us are perfect but at this time in my life I was as near the image of *God* as anyone could be.  I did not think of myself in that way but I know it was true and even *Jesus* was challenged at times to know what *God* wanted him to do.  I studied the Bible daily and before I was twelve I had read all or most of it.  And it was my wish to become a minister and teach the word of *God.*  So I was indeed pure of heart in my faith and I thought *God* had something in mind for me and I was here for a special purpose.  Being a Christian and following the scriptures was very difficult in the days that *Jesus* walked among us, and it has not gotten any easier.

I read from the Bible, John 2:14 where *Jesus* went to the Temple and ran out the *money changers,* etc.

*" And Jesus found in the Temple those that sold oxen, sheep and doves, and the changers of money, and when he had made a scourge of small cords, he drove them out of the Temple, and the sheep, and the oxen; and poured out the changers money, and overthrew the tables ".* I felt I should get a stick and go to church and chastise and at least threaten to run out the so called leaders of our church, the Deacons that got their positions by being large contributors to the church's building fund, etc. These Deacons made no effort at helping the poor in our community thou they had so much. It had become clear to me that one of the goals of the church was to increase their wealth or *"building fund"* to enlarge the church and beautify the exterior and the interior. This was a good investment because the masses seem to flock to churches that were luxurious and beautiful. Larger congregations add more to the church's coffers and so it goes. Does anyone care about the principles that *Christ* taught us? These *"Temples"* we are building are being worshiped instead of *God*.

As a young Christian as close to Christ as a person could be, I knew the church was not following his teaching. Acceptable degrees of sin made being a Christian a right of ascension upon entering the church and the largest tithe seem to pay off a larger degree of sin. But worse, they seemed to take leadership rolls that sometimes surpassed the roll of the Pastor. He came to the church with a great faith throughout his life, only to end here being a financial overseer of the Building Fund.

Reverend Thompson was a good man and meant well. He did go on from this church to the Seminary in Atlanta where he taught for many years and was well respected by all that knew him. But at this time I knew what his answer would be before I asked him. I wanted to take that job because we needed the money even though I knew it was a sin to work on the Sabbath. That was my trial and I failed but I would not have taken the job if Preacher Thompson had told me it was a sin and I should not. I believe that. But I knew before I asked what the answer would be. And so he failed *Christ* and me that day. But as a mature Christian today, I realize that Christians may fail *Christ* many times and still be Chistians and on Judgement Day we must answer for our failures.

The job with Mr. Bob lasted several years and became a big part of my childhood and formative young adult years. It was certainly like an extended family. Every morning he picked me up at my house a little after 4:15 am and we headed for the paper station to fold papers and to count out papers to each of the bicycle boys. Then all of us like a team went to the White House Restaurant for our coffee and donuts. It was very much like a family after awhile. Then Mr. Bob and I started out with his Plymouth loaded down with papers and me on the running board on the passenger side with the window down. On cold mornings I could at least stick my head and shoulders inside to break the cold air. As we turned a corner I would jump off with three or four papers in my hand and deliver them to houses on that street, then jump back on at the corner to await the next grouping of deliveries. Some single houses standing along would just get the paper tossed to them as we passed. The degree of service depended on how many complaints we had received for wet or torn deliveries. Bob would keep me informed on that you can be sure.

I enjoyed the job actually and it was only the starting time that got to me sometimes. By the time I got off the route and made it to school I was exhausted and sleepy. Many times the first period I would lay my head on my desk and take a nap. The teachers were sympathetic. They did not give me particularly good grades but they did not hassle me either.

Over time I had told Mr. Bob that I would like to take over a bicycle route when one became available.

After about two years one of the boys moved away and I was given his route. It was a good one - 170 customers - about half on dirt streets which are harder pedaling on a bicycle, and about half black customers. I mention that only because it was my first real close up interaction with blacks. This was a totally segregated time. They did not attend our schools or our churches and usually did not live real close bye except where some poor whites might get real close to the all black areas. We had not been in that situation even though we were as poor as you could get. So it was a real learning experience for me. Later in life I would realize how beneficial this experience was in many of my future jobs. Collecting the paper on Sunday was sometimes difficult and I learned fast that if they did not pay Sunday morning, I did not leave the paper with *"Hambone"* inside that they badly wanted. When I refused to leave the Sunday, they would usually recount their resources and come up with my thirty-five cents. If they did not, I kept the Sunday paper and tried to sell it along the way or on the corner when I was through for fifteen cents which recovered half my weekly expense. Usually they would pay me again during the week to get their paper started again. I got along well with them and my white customers on the route. I learned the basic lesson in business, genuinely care for your customers and they will know it and be loyal to you.

I continued the paper route about two more years, so I worked for Mr. Bob a total of about four. We were continuing to make things work as a family. We had a little money coming in from each of the children at home: Bobbie worked part time and went to school as did Vince and me. Little Robert remained sickly - not bed ridden but very under weight and fairly inactive. Events continued to balance out the changes in our life. I was making more but Claudia had left with her new husband, but John had joined the Navy. He wasn't old enough but he went to the Adele, Georgia courthouse and got Bobbie's birth certificate and forged his name onto it. Our birth certificates were completed as *"Baby Taylor"*, born this date, etc. to Oscar Taylor and Ovieda Belle Taylor, so it was fairly easy to change them. So, John went into the Navy just after World War II ended and was off to China on an "LST" Ship. He made out an allotment check to Mama as a dependent so we received a small check each month from the Navy.

It just seemed that events would fall into place like that for us. John's check took the place of what we had gotten from Claudia while she was home with my niece Becky. So we were okay, dysfunctional, but doing fine. Each of us bought our own clothes, shoes, etc as we needed them and paid our school expenses and none of these items came from the household money. Then we gave Mama what we could to buy food and rent, but now we had a steady income from John's allotment check to take care of the rent and some basic items. Vince was working at a bank as a "courier" after school. He delivered bank transfers between other banks and businesses. He eventually dropped out of school at fifteen years old. He did not like school and wasn't much of a student. He was a great boxer and the president of the bank was a big sportsman and liked to sponsor him in his boxing career. He fought as an amateur for the Valdosta Boys Club Boxing Team. He would go on to win the Georgia State Golden Gloves Boxing Title in the lightweight division in 1947. Then he won the welterweight title in Florida in 1948. Then in 1950 he joined the U.S. Marines and won the Middleweight Championship of the 2nd Marines Division. He was truly a great boxer but that career was ended by injuries incurred in the Korean War.

The next major change in our lives would occur in 1950 when Mama decided to marry Gus Mathis and move with him to Jacksonville, Florida. They had begun a relationship over the past year while he was renting a room in the boarding house over our rental apartment. The job he was on in Valdosta was ending and his union had placed him back in Jacksonville on a new job and he had to go. Mama did not want him to leave her. She thought it was her chance to have a normal family again, a husband and a father for Robert and me. The others were grown now. Vince had already decided to join the Marines and enter the war just starting in Korea. Bobbie had married Lamar Thompson about this time in Valdosta.

So again everything seemed to be falling into place at the same time. It seemed to me to be a good thing. I was very tired of the early morning job and school and at times just felt total exhaustion. I hoped Mama would be happier and I thought a normal home would be good for Robert. We all liked Gus a lot. So one day just like that we all packed up and moved to Jacksonville, Florida.

In the beginning it was rough for us in Jacksonville. We had stored our furniture in Valdosta and rented a furnished apartment in Jacksonville and it was not as nice as what we had in Valdosta. That seemed to embarrass Mama. I did not have a job and we were uprooted and in a strange city in a low-class apartment. But I did not have to get up at 4:00 o'clock in the morning - and we did not really have that much in Valdosta to miss. So I felt pretty good about the move. Jacksonville was a big city and you could sense that it did not have the cast system that was ever present in a small southern town like Valdosta. It was more of a melting pot of different kinds people and I liked it better. Soon Gus got out and found us a house to rent out on the edge of town. A whole house of our own for the first time in many years and with a large yard and a creek way back about three hundred-yards where we could go fishing! Gus and me built us a fishing boat in the back yard over the next few months. He was very good to all of us. Robert seemed to do a lot better and accepted Gus as his daddy without a problem. Of course I was too old for that but I liked him fine. He was a hard working *"union man"* and I learned a lot from him. John had got out of the service and came and lived with us for awhile and worked at a department store. Before long he got married and moved out and it was just the four of us again. I worked some with Gus as a plumber's helper and did some painting and cleaning up houses for our landlord who had known Gus for years. He paid me fifty cents per hour. It was enough to have my own spending money and buy some clothes.

Somehow now I did not feel like an integral part of anything. It may sound strange, but for years I had to work along with the rest of the family to survive and I was accustomed to that role. Now Gus was the breadwinner and he was a hard worker. Mama did not need me. She loved me but she did not need me. I did not like school, which I guess is not really strange for someone my age, but I did not have a roll model to instill in me the need to graduate and continue my education. I decided to quit school and join the Navy. So I talked to a Navy Recruiter and he signed me up, subject to Mama's permission because I was only seventeen on my birthday - March 15th - which was just a few weeks away. This year would have been my high school graduation but I had fallen behind and would not have graduated. This was when public school lasted eleven years. I was disappointed that I would have to go to school another year and the recruiter told me I could finish through programs the Navy had. Mama finally agreed with Gus pushing her because he was an Army Veteran from World War I and was very patriotic. He thought all young men should go into the service. After I got in, I might say that I would agree with him if the term were one to two years - but not four years. Believe me that is a long time to be in the military.

The Navy was another big change in my life. There were a lot of people there but not a family, no love, just a job to do when you were told to do it. Then go to bed when they told you to and get up when they told you. You had three meals a day without fail, housing and clothing furnished, and a small salary. After all I had been through in my life, I needed this for awhile.

I did not have to worry about Mama and Robert because I was convinced Gus would take good care of them. In fact, in 1952 Mama got the biggest joy of her life I think when she and Gus signed the papers to buy their very own home! It was the first home she had ever owned and it made her very happy. She would eventually die in that same home and would not have had it any other way. That was thirty-two years later. To me that time period is so relative after all the pain and suffering she endured for many years in Adele and Valdosta, Georgia. She ended her life living in this home she owned with a husband that loved her for a longer period of time and she was very happy. *"The meek shall inherit the earth".* Perhaps God can sometimes find a shepherd and a small patch of land for one of his flock on earth.

I think so because it was almost like Gus just appeared one day and Mama met him. We are talking about someone who never worked and hardly ever left the house even to go shopping. What would be the odds of her finding a husband in a roomer from the Gentlemen's Boarding House upstairs from our apartment. And the man was almost as quite and introverted as she was. She deserved a break, some happiness here on earth, and Gus came along at just the time. This was not like rags to riches, it was just a little house on the edge of town with a hard working *"union man"* to live out their lives together. He also died in this little house some twenty years after they bought it. I'm sure they will both experience the golden streets in heaven but will always remember with love this little house and their time together on earth.

Robert got better as he grew older and Gus got him a job with a friend who owned a repair garage and a used car lot. Robert only went to public school to the sixth grade because of his health, so he needed to learn a trade. This job was a trade out Gus made with his friend, no salary but teach him the mechanics trade. After awhile he started paying him and said he was the best mechanic, bodyman and painter he had ever had. He raced stockcars and was very good at that as well. Fate dealt us a terrible blow when he was drafted into the Army at twenty-one and had just married. The army sent him to Lawton, Oklahoma and he took his wife, Jean. They lived off base in an apartment and he bought a motor scooter to ride back and forth on. He was hit by a drunk driver and killed just a few months after being drafted and with his wife pregnant.

That was the saddest moment of my life. It was just so unfair after being sickly most of his life and finally coming out of that and having some real successes for such a short time. But I thanked God for giving him that period of his life that was rich and made him happy and complete before he had to go. How long you live is maybe not as important as how you live and how happy you are while you live. I believe that. Thank you *God.*

## THE ADULT TAYLORS

The question at the beginning was "How would this kind of fear and torture effect the physical and the mental health of these poor folks?" One might also wonder how another generation or two might be affected.

Well, the answer was probably what a psychologist would have perceived. The distrust of society that was etched into the minds of these children, the failures of their Father, the effects of undernourishment, the lack of positive roll models, all would be devastating to their growth and mental health. First, as a result of the influence of these factors, only one, Claudia Belle graduated from high school. Bobbie left school in the tenth grade to take a full time job. All the boys served in the military, which was a sign of the times. In our modern drug culture some may have ended up doing prison time instead. But the military was an escape mechanism of that time and that does not infer that patriotism did not also play a roll in their decision. There would be other escape attempts, always trying to distance themselves from what seemed to them to be an unforgiving, uncaring society.

The absence of effective roll models is very damaging to children trying to climb out of the ghettos. When they look around and find no family members with high school diplomas, no one that ever attended college, no one that ever gained economic status above minimal levels, it is easy for them to accept those levels as their goals. The short term economic gain of full time employment is attractive and attracts many away from education.

Bobbie left high school for a full time job and was quite successful over the next few years, moving up to Office Manager positions. She was smart and industrious. School had all the weight of social problems that were not as visible in the work place where everyone was judged by the quality of the work performed for their employer. She later married and had two children. Her husband, Lamar Thompson was a hard working automobile mechanic at the local Chevrolet dealership. He was considered their best and made very good money for a mechanic at that time, but Bobbie had a problem with money. She wanted to be somebody that she was not, a socialite and a person of some means. Surely this was a reflection of all the years of being dirt poor. Now she wanted more - now - to show *"them"* that she was somebody. Looking back now, it is very sad. She would go to the most expensive Boutiques in Valdosta, and we only had a couple that could get close to assuming that role, and open charge accounts. Then once or twice a month she would go shopping and take out three or four dresses for approval that cost more each than Lamar made in a week. When he would ask her where the hell she would wear such expensive dresses, even if she could afford them, she would just put him down. She would like to wear them to the Country Club if he was not such a miserable failure and a redneck mechanic! She would buy some of these dresses and he would work weekends on side jobs to pay for them. Then he would buy a pint or two of whiskey and get drunk. The poor man's escape when he can't think of the answers. After awhile they reached the point that they just could not stand each other anymore.

In my heart I know Bobbie was suffering from psychological impairments caused by those years of abject poverty and hunger. She wanted to rise to that level she had looked up at for so many years. She did not have anyone that she respected to hold her hand and guide her in taking small, deliberate steps up a very steep hill. She needed someone to council her to enjoy her family and make that journey something they could all enjoy. She did not have that roll model so she put them all through hell until the break-up. She was divorced and became a working mother, taking care of her two children, Scott and Steve (Sparky) as best she could for many years with some child support from Lamar. He died a young man at fifty-eight from liver disease (probably cancer). Bobbie lived out her life without ever knowing much success with her dreams of wealth. Her wealthiest days were when she was with Lamar and her two boys in their nice little home in Valdosta but she could not see it because of her demons.

Bobbie died in an accident June 1, 1988 while visiting her son, Scott in California. A second-generation story is her son Scott, after graduating from high school in Jacksonville, Florida; he joined the Air Force and was stationed in California. He continued his education and found employment in California after the Air Force in county government as a manager and has been very successful. Unfortunately the younger son Steve died a violent death at the age of 17 which was never completely solved. He was the victim of the broken home and lack of roll models and came to a sad end not uncommon in the inter-city of Jacksonville.

John returned home after serving in the Navy and the Marine Corp. and joined us in Jacksonville. He attended business school on the G I Bill and got his high school diploma while working for Furchott's Department Store as a salesman. He had some of the same financial problems as Bobbie had, the dreams of rapidly ascending the social ladder when it was not possible and took some falls. He never had a problem with alcohol though and that was a blessing. He was a talented salesman and much smarter than the level of his education would have dictated. He progressed in the retail field working for Sears as a Department Manager and then to Wards as a Merchandise Regional

Manager over a thirty-year span. He was successful and showed little psychological damage as a result of his childhood except the need to keep up with *"the Jones"* when it was not possible. But I think a lot of folks suffer from that affliction. John had two children, Johnny and Jeffrey with his first wife, Marie. He then had a daughter, Kirstie, with his second wife, Alice. All lived middle-class lives and were reasonably happy as far as I could determine. We were not particularly close, as was the case with the other siblings one to the other for whatever reasons.

Vince and I were the closest of any two of the children. We were two years apart in age and we both boxed at the Valdosta Boy's Club - although there was no comparison in our talent level. Vince was a great amateur boxer. We were both in the service at the same time, me in the Navy while he was a Marine during the Korean War. He would write me from Korea and tell me about the hell the Marines were enduring. I felt good that I had joined the Navy and we were in a back-up position to the Marines, but I knew it was way back. He had landed at Inchon with the 2nd Marine Division and was fighting a close up war against overwhelming numerical odds. He was wounded once and moved back to a hospital ship. In a few weeks when he was recovered, he was sent back to the front line. I think that did not happen in any other war. But the North Koreans and the Red Chinese were pouring into South Korea in hoard numbers and we needed every man that could fire a weapon. Vince was wounded again in the leg and foot and sent back to the Hospital Ship and eventually home. He would receive *two Purple Hearts* and the *Bronze Star* and a lot of horrible memories of killing possibly hundreds of swarming Koreans and Chinese - all human beings no matter what we thought about their politics and their intentions at the time.

I will never know how much the Korean War experiences effected Vince or how much of his eventual mental problems where the result of his childhood and social bewilderment. I do believe though that he had more problems than the Marines ever cared to admit. They had lots of wounded coming home and they were processing them as quickly as possible and discharging them. He was sent to the Naval Air Station Hospital at Jacksonville, Florida where he would stay several months. He received treatment for his wounds and then they realized he had some psychological problems as well. In different times he would have received more treatment. They referred to him as suffering from "*passive aggressive Psychosis*" but made little attempt at treatment and did not include it as part of his permanent disability. Bones in his foot were permanently damaged and he was deemed to be ten percent disabled. To me it seemed he was schizophrenic at the time of his discharge and he would deteriorate over the years. He said he heard voices talking to him way back then. I am not a psychiatrist but he was sick when he came back from Korea and should have been given more treatment then and should have been classified one hundred percent disable. None of that though in fact, would have probably had much effect on the continuation of his mental problems to their ultimate conclusion.

Years later when his condition deteriorated and he became delusional after Mama died and he was living alone in her house, the veteran's hospital did take him in and cared for him. He was transferred to a full nursing care center where he remained for several years not knowing much of anything until his death. I grieved for him while he was alive and I grieved for him at his death. That is all I could ever do for him. He suffered many years and his wife and family along with him for sure. His wife, Ruth finally divorced him and moved closer to her family along with their children, Ovieda, Rebecca, Vince Jr., and Teresa. She worked and cared for the children. I did not see them for many years until the funeral. He was sixty-six at his death and all the children were grown and took care of all the arrangements. They were all fine children and loved their father very much. I am certain he loved them just as much. The U.S. Marines were informed of his death and sent a Color Guard for a full military funeral with a rifle salute when he was buried. He certainly deserved it and his family felt pride along with our sorrow.

After returning home to Valdosta for about two years, Claudia met a First Lieutenant from Moody Air Force Base, Jimmy Bohan and they were married. He was from Texas and looked and acted like what I thought a Texan would. He was over six feet tall, drove a new Lincoln convertible smiled a lot and was a little on the loud side. But he was a great person. Everyone liked him a lot. He was a hero for his many bombing runs over Germany and had a box full of medals including the *"Distinguished Flying Cross"* but was not a career soldier. He wanted out as soon as possible. Claudia wanted him to stay. She loved the glamour and aristocracy of being an officer's wife and did not want it to end. She finally prevailed; he re-listed and was transferred to MacDill Air Force Base, Tampa, Florida. They moved taking Becky with them, which broke Mama's heart. She had come to believe that Becky was always going to stay with her because of the divorce and she had cared for her since she was born. Mama never really got over this. It may seem surreal to someone else, but she really thought Becky was hers - as if she was an orphan she had taken in because her daddy did not want her and Claudia had left her with Mama for such a long time - although she did come back to see her every few weeks and paid for her care. She loved Becky with all her heart just as if she had given birth to her. Claudia would not return for ten years and even then it was never the same with them.

Sometime later about 1949 - Claudia would meet a Captain Clark Aubel at MacDill, divorced Jimmy and married him. Prior to her divorce she had another daughter, Susan Aubel. I don't know what happened to Jimmy after that but I know he was discharged from the

Air Force and went back to Texas. I wish him well for he was a real American Hero and a very nice person.

Claudia married Clark Aubel in 1950 and they remained married until her death in July 2003. Clark was a good Father to the two daughters as they moved around the world as Clark continued his Air Force career for twenty-eight years, retiring as a Colonel. Claudia was an Officer's wife for all these years and on into retirement. She was very happy and lived what was to her a dream life.

Many times over the years I thought of her and imagined her at the Officer's Club, Dinners and Parties on the Air Force Bases in Japan, California and Alaska as the Colonels' Wife. When asked about her home and family back in Georgia, I always imagined that she would tell them that she grew up on a plantation. The real story of living in a corn barn before she went away to nursing school and the poverty from which she came had long since been buried wherever people bury such things. Instead she would tell them of the hundreds of white-faced Herefords grazing on thousand of acres; her horse named Wonder and her dog Dolly. Why not? She deserved those memories to go along with her position as a Colonels' wife. Over the years she came to believe it all, I imagine, though that was not her intent in the beginning. And, if indeed she did dream a life up to go with her success as an officer's wife no one should begrudge her that. My memories of these times remain vivid; the rats in the corn shack, the snakes under the shack, the hunger, the social rejection, the years of child labor, the family sticking together, the happiness, the faith in God, the disappointments, the victories, all a kaleidoscope of my life which is now me. I need to know me - I want to write poetry, tell stories, and paint pictures that have soul and to do those things, I first have to know who I am. Creative visions will not do, you must expose yourself and immerse yourself in all the muck life has put you through, then cleanse your spirit and go forward as if born again while retaining all the memories. To do less is to retain all the self-protecting, defensive lies we tell ourselves to make life acceptable. Now you can see life and death with clarity and fear neither.

Daddy lived the balance of his life in Valdosta and was close to Bobbie and her sons after she divorced Lamar and lived on in Valdosta for awhile. Bobbie eventually moved to Jacksonville to be closer to Mama and then Daddy was the only one left in Valdosta. He had a small barbershop but was primarily a professional gambler the last twenty years of his life. He never acquired a lot of money but was not poor. At some point he had stopped drinking and improved as a person after that. He was a heavy smoker - chain-smoking *"Lucky Strikes"* and even stronger *"Home Run"* cigarettes. That would eventually be the cause of his death from throat cancer at the age of sixty-five. All the children except Claudia had made peace with him over the years and loved him. We all attended his funeral in Valdosta in 1965, including Mama. I think we all came full circle that day. There was no hate left. We had all moved on with our lives and what we had gone through was accepted as part of bad times. We were all trying to find our place now - none of us in Valdosta and none of us wanted to ever be there again. But it was not Valdosta's fault either. I think we all knew we had to take our demons and go forward with them and do the best we are capable of doing. Successes and failures would follow but each of us would have to take responsibility for them.

My life was uneventful after discharge from the Navy at twenty-one years of age. I was just one of many thousands of veterans returning from the Korean War. The four years in the Navy gave me time to reflect on my childhood and my concerns about my ability to find my way in this society. I had found my way well enough in the Navy - I attended two schools during the first two years of my service then spent the last two years in California and a seaplane squadron in the Philippines. That experience broadened my knowledge of the world situation a great deal. I was *"my daddy's son"* as my Mama used to say. I was a drinker and a carouser to be sure, but I was dependable and a hard worker and therefore successful in each of the jobs I found after my discharge.

I married Carolyn during the first year back and worked at the A & P Food Store in Jacksonville, Florida. After a year or so, I went to work for a small loan company as a field collector - a rough job that only paid $250.00 per month for very long hours. I worked hard because I had a family and needed more money and wanted a promotion. I was promoted to Office Manager of a new Aetna Finance Company office when I was twenty-four years old. I continued in this business for a total of twelve years. With this background and some financial classes at St. Petersburg College, I landed a job with Mack Truck's Inc., which was a Fortune 400 Company at that time. I did well in that job and went on to become a District Manager and then Regional Manager for them in Knoxville, Tennessee, San Francisco, and finally Chicago. So, I was a Regional Manager of three of their five regions over several years.

I was proud of my success considering where I came from, I was good at what I did and had work ethics that were second to none.

During this period, my daughter Linda graduated from California State with a Bachelor Degree in English. She would eventually teach school in Florida. My son Kerry graduated on the Dean's list from the University of Tennessee School of Business. He became a successful Real Estate Broker in Ft. Lauderdale, Florida. My daughter Teresa followed me to Mack Trucks working for the Charlotte, North Carolina Branch for fifteen years. Later she would move to Florida to be close to the family and worked many years for the Bic Corporation in Clearwater, Florida as a Regional Secretary. My daughter Carol Jean married young to Keith Wilks in Columbia, South Carolina and have my only grandchildren, Jessica, Brandon, and Taylor. I am very proud of them all. I think this is pretty good for the next generation after the *"Bottom Feeders"* survived Adele and Valdosta, Georgia.

I don't want to give the impression that I eased through life without any problems. That was not the case, I tried to fail many times. I drank too much - deep inside I knew I deserved to fail -it was in my blood. I had a bad disposition and made my wife and children miserable many times. I needed a lot of help and a lot of understanding from my wife, my children and my mother. Something deep inside kept reminding me that I had lived through hell and that I owed my family and myself something better. Maybe it was *God* keeping an eye on one of the meek that could enter Heaven if only he did not get lost.

It was up to me to be the roll model that I never had as a child. But it was a constant battle because failure comes almost as the natural order of things when you grow up in a failed society. So, I do understand why most with my background would ultimately fail. Over the years I slowly learned how to visualize myself as the dominant person that I am. The person that could lead my family and my employees to be more than they thought they could be. I knew I was more than I once thought I was and now I learned to project that to others. At fifty years old I took early retirement from Mack Financial and wished them well. They had become like an extended family to me and had given me many opportunities over the years but I wanted to do something that would allow me to do more creative things.

In my later years I became a Real Estate Broker,

an Artist, and a Poet. I made a good living selling real estate while not feeling that I had to be anything or anyone that I was not. With a corporation like Mack, creativity is stifled to a large extent because you are required to march in step with a corporate plan and a corporate image and that is how it should be in that environment. I look back now and realize that for most of my life I was acting. I was a good actor and could play the roles I was given - as a collector for a small loan company and as their manager but it was not really me. Then I took the role as a Finance Manager and as a Regional Finance Manager for Mack Truck, Inc. and I was allowed to direct and to act. They gave me the end goals but I was allowed to direct the play. I became more and more confident that I could do anything, play any part, and then one day in Chicago, I decided to write myself out of the play and it was surreal how everyone accepted that and we said goodbye and I was gone. I never looked back; it was just a part.

I wanted something different for the rest of my life. I just wanted to be me with no one else setting goals for me to attain for them. A real estate salesman is a free lance entrepreneur that uses his personality to attract customers to use his services. Your mind remains clear and uncluttered by this activity. I found that I could write poetry or paint at the same time and so I did and my life became enriched. I did not say I became rich. I had already moved beyond that when I made the decision to leave Mack. Now my search was for clarity and quality.

The goal for all of us should be to work in whatever way we can to be sure that children in the United States do not go to bed hungry tonight. I pray that the churches in the United States will work to establish "*Domestic Missionaries*" to search out children and families that need help. When I was growing up in Adele, Georgia in third world conditions, the Baptist Church, Presbyterians, Mormons, Catholics, and others had large missionary expeditions all over the world. They ministered to the poor and under- privileged of foreign countries but none of them found us or the other thousands starving in the United States. The government finally found us when a doctor told them we came to him for medical care. Then we found the Presbyterian Church after the Welfare Department moved us near to it. The faith and prayers that we received from the Presbyterian Church had a large influence on us and gave us the strength of faith to survive those difficult years. That faith through prayer that helped was not offered in a proactive way to thousands of Americans during those years and I feel many churches should pray for forgiveness. Then they should go forth searching for desperate families in their area and minister to them when found. *God* will smile on you and these meek folks may lead you to heaven.

*Gene Taylor*

# EPILOGUE

**"The Bottom Feeders"** tells a story of despair, poverty, religion, and the opportunities found in America. In writing this story of our struggles, losses and victories, certain truths became evident. As an example, it became evident to me that the psychological damage of living at the low rung of a cast system was the most injurious of all the pains we endured. Having said that, one must also assume that other factors could have lifelong effects, such as undernourishment as an infant and even prenatal, may have effected brain size, intelligence, learning ability and eventually education.

Of course education or the lack thereof, has profound effects on earning potential and the educational opportunities of the following generations. However the psychological problems that manifest themselves are the most crippling, it would seem. As you struggle to prove yourself and climb out of the ghetto, the need to fail is overwhelming. It has been so etched into your psyche that you are a low-life and doomed to remain so, that failure becomes the anticipated result.

There is no doubt that religion not only played a large roll in the lives of the Taylor family, but also that they might not have survived without it. The strength necessary to maintain the family while digging unharvested potatoes for food while living in an abandoned shack could not have been found without their Mother having enormous faith in *God*. She taught the children to have faith that *God* would provide throughout their ordeal, they never doubted *God*. They may have wondered about some of their relatives, some of the community, and the churches in the area, but never *God*. This gave them the strength to survive, but even more it gave them statue. They were part of *Gods family* and they were the meek that would inherit the *Kingdom of God*. Their Mama taught this to them and read it to them from the Bible and they never doubted it.

They knew there would be a way and there was always a way.

So this is a story of religion as much as anything. Immigrants leaving Europe and England to escape Religious intolerance settled America. In America they found religious freedom along with almost unbearable conditions that turned out to be a perfect match. Without their religion and faith that *God* would protect them from the elements, the hunger, and the other dangers, they could not have survived. They survived, their faith was greatly reinforced and they became more deeply religious. This is the very foundation of our country.

Over the years, America became a melting pot of races and religions, and some with no religion, but the base remained one of strong religious beliefs. Sometimes, when fate dealt them a very bad situation, they found they had the faith to guide them and the strength they otherwise would not have had. That was where the Taylors found themselves. They were in situations as bad as those faced by the early settlers but without the friends. It seemed they had no friends at times except *God*. Just imagine what they would have done without him. Imagine how close they must have become - would not you give anything to become that close to *God*? You can, without flirting with starvation, without living in a shack without lights or heat, without being ostracized by society, if you go one on one with *God* and tell him you need a friend, not a handout, but a friend to talk to and to believe in. When you need someone to talk to, he will be there. You have to help yourself. You have to dig your own potatoes and cut your own firewood, but he will be there with you and he will protect you. With him, you will find happiness - without him, you may do many things and be the envy of many, but you cannot find happiness. Remember you can find *God* in many places. You don't have to look very far because he is with you now as he has always been.

Make contact and you will begin to control the problems in your life that have prevented you from being happy. Remember that happiness is not always entwined with wealth. I sometimes think we lose *God* and happiness the same day regardless of our financial position in life.

*Hello God, I'm still here!*

*Gene Taylor*

*2003*

# The Bottom Feeders
## (Some call us white trash)

'The Bottom Feeders' delivers several messages in a fast format with no frills. First, it is a sad story of a very poor family during the depression years of the 1930's and the early 1940's. Then it is a motivational story of how the Taylor family is self-sufficient and able to survive and improve their situation through hard work.

More than anything else, it is a religious book. Without their strong religious beliefs for strength, their very survival would have been in doubt. However, the story is more than survival. It is a story of love for family and *God* as if they were one. A story of happiness because of that love.

It is a story everyone should share with his or her family.

H. Gene Taylor

Author

# About the Author

Gene Taylor, born in Adele, Georgia in 1934, retired from Mack Trucks, semi retired from A Better Way Realty, Inc. his real estate brokerage, now spends most of his time painting, writing poetry, and children's books. All have religious themes, not by conscious design but more like he was wired that way many years ago.

www.ingramcontent.com/pod-product-compliance
Lightning Source LLC
Chambersburg PA
CBHW030352290526
45785CB00004B/1712